ONE

UNDERSTANDING TERRITORIAL LOCKS

Every territory – heavenly, earthly, physical, spiritual, named and unnamed, seen and unseen, land, air, sea, organised, developed, incorporated or not; belong to The Lord God Almighty. It is He who holds the whole of creation in His hands. He alone has full, total and complete authority over the entire heavens, earth and the universe.

It pleased God in His sovereignty to give the earth territory – air, sea and land to mankind; for man to display God's glory, and manifest God's reality.

And God said, let us make man in our own image and after our likeness, and let them have dominion over the fowl of the air, and over the fish of the sea, over the cattle and over every living thing that moves on the land.- Genesis 1:26

The heavens are the LORD'S, but the earth he has given to the human race. – Psalm 115:16

Engaging Territorial Locks

The enemy of mankind puts restrictions over territories to hinder and to obstruct the manifestations of the Living God. Territorial locks are put over the inheritance of mankind so that man would not manifest the fullness of God's glory and power. Contrary spirits (territorial spirits) are set over territories to restrain a land, a people, a sphere of influence, a field of speciality, lives, destinies and much more; so as to prevent them from aligning with the perfect plans and purposes of God. The enemy in a bid to work against God, places a strict restraint on a territory so that the territory will not fulfil God.

Territorial spirits (familiar spirits, witchcraft and sorcery, satanic powers, etc.), seek to rule over territories so as to subdue, to manipulate, to hinder, to harm and to control the lives and destinies of men. Territorial spirits exercise power of ownership over people and locations; to draw them to self, to sin, to satan, so as to cut them off completely from the voice and from the influence of God.

A territory is - a life, a destiny, a specified atmosphere, a corporate environment, a location, a sphere of influence, a field of interest, a group of people, a specified entity, an organised area, a group or unit, a city, a country, a continent, etc.

Any territory that is under the control, the influence, the ruler-ship or the restraint and constraint of a territorial spirit/s, is under occupation. **The plan of the enemy is to occupy a territory and turn it into a reproach and an abhorrence unto the Lord God Almighty.**

Territorial locks are curses. A curse is a stronghold, that is, a fortified powerhouse of devastating and catastrophic occurrences. A curse is an invocation of tragedy, a supernatural summoning of ill will. Any territory that carries a curse has been shackled to misfortune and locked down to adversity.

Territorial locks manifest as works of darkness operating in and within a territory to put that territory under the influence of darkness and thereby prevent the manifestation of the will of God in that space. Works of darkness like magic, tricks and pranks, witchcraft, sorcery, occultism, blood sacrifices, demon worship, all manner of abominations; are deliberate operations of the kingdom of darkness to hinder the move and the expression of God, to keep a territory occupied by and for darkness.

Territorial locks also manifest as works of the flesh; negative and wrong mentality, desires and thoughts that are contrary to God, unbelief and doubt, distrust in God, complacency, laziness in the things of God, lovelessness, being wise in your own eyes, pride, selfishness, foolishness, lusts, self aggrandizement, greed, stubbornness, disobedience, rebellion, prayerlessness and so on.

All features, activities and manifestations that dishonour God, that glorify sin, satan and self are territorial locks. They are deliberate works of darkness to secure a territory (a life, a space, an area, an entity, etc.) for destruction.

Why Unlock?

To unlock is to free from restraint or restrictions. Unlocking a territory is freeing the territory from the restraints, the restrictions, the influence and the control of sin, satan and self. To unlock a territory is to destroy the plans and purposes of all illegal and contrary forces over that territory, so that the plans and purposes of God can be made manifest therein.

To unlock is to open. Unlocking a territory is to open a territory; to the power, the presence, the plans and the purposes of the Living God.

To unlock is to undo. To unlock a territory is to undo the evil works, the negative influence and the power of sin, satan and self over a particular entity; thereby bringing into manifestation the fulfilment of the perfect will of God.

To unlock is to restore. To unlock a territory is to restore the territory to the original owner, the original settings, the original plans and purposes. To unlock a territory is to restore the territory (i.e. a location, a community, a life, a specified entity, etc...) to the excellence of God.

To unlock a territory is to furnish a key to a particular location or sphere. To unlock a territory is to remove and to undo all that had shut and locked the territory off to the fulfilment of the thoughts of God.

To unlock is to bless. To Bless means – to empower to succeed. To unlock a territory is to release that territory from curses into the fullness of the blessings of God. A territory unlocked, is a territory blessed; that is - empowered unto the favour, the protection, the power, the glory and the pleasure of God. Unlocking a territory brings that territory into all the goodness and benefits that are found in God.

Unlocking a territory establishes that territory in the governance, the authority, the influence and the glory of Jehovah God.

Keys unlock and lock

Keys have the power to open locks and to also close locks. Keys are answers, solutions, remedies. A key provides entry, it gives access. To unlock a territory, a key or keys are given to enter into the territory and to open it up for solutions and answers.

When a key to a territory is provided, there is bona fide access and legal entry. **A key gives resolutions, remedies and cures.**

Keys also mean freedom. Keys symbolise knowledge. Keys give freedom of access and knowledge of entry to a territory. A territory under the control and influence of sin, satan and self is a territory in bondage. The keys of a territory provide liberty and deliverance for the territory. **A key provides for a territory - the**

entry of the will of God, the access of the perfect intention of the Almighty.

A key is a symbol of power and authority, a symbol of ease. A key gives power of access. A key gives a bona fide, legal entry into a territory. Possession of the key means possession of **authority and ease of access**. "Possession of the key" means – "no struggles" concerning access or entry.

Where To And How To Obtain The Key/s of a Territory

The territories of the heavens and the earth belong to the Almighty God of all creation.

To the lord your God belong the heavens even the highest heavens and the earth and everything in it. Deuteronomy 10:12

So you may know that the whole Earth is the Lord's. Exodus 9:29

The earth is the LORD'S, and all it contains, The world, and those who dwell in it. Psalm 24:1

The Almighty God is the Creator of all things, He is Lord and King over all, His Name is Jesus. He is the Word through whom all things consist and were created. However, there are spheres, fields, lives and destinies, locations - indeed various territories where Jesus Christ is not received and acknowledged as "Lord and King over all". In such territories where the authority and governance of Jesus Christ is not received, acknowledged and proclaimed; territorial spirits hold away as illegal occupants and oppressors over such territories.

In any territory (life, destiny, space, field, sphere, location, area, city, country, continent, etc.) where there is the spiritual, physical, full manifestation of the sovereign ruler-ship and complete dominion of God the Father, God the son and God the Holy Spirit; right there is the manifestation of the Kingdom of God. On the inside of Jehovah God lies the answers, the solutions, the power, the authority, the knowledge to restore any and every territory to His pattern.

Territorial Sovereignty

The Owner of the territories of the heavens and the earth has the full possession of the keys of the territories. The Creator of all that we see and we do not see is the bona fide, inarguable Owner of the heavens and indeed of the whole earth, His Name is Jesus. Jesus is the King, the ruler, the Owner over the territories of the heavens and the earth. **Jesus Christ has territorial sovereignty** over the territories of the heavens and the earth.

All things have been handed over to me by my Father, and no one knows the Son except the Father, and no one knows the Father except the Son and anyone to whom the Son chooses to reveal him. Matthew 11:27

Unlocking The Territories – Restoring The Order Of God

To unlock a territory is to restore the territory to the original settings. The ruler-ship of God, the governance of God, the authority and the sovereignty of God over the territories of the heavens and the earth is the original settings of all territories.

The will of God, the thoughts of Jesus Christ, the plans and purposes of God is the original settings of the territories of all creation. The Lordship and the Supremacy of Jesus Christ are the original settings of all the territories (i.e. the realms of God, the realms and the spheres of men, the lives and the destinies of all mankind).

To unlock a territory, a key is required; not just any key, but the correct key. How does one identify the correct keys with which to unlock the various territories?

TWO

IDENTIFYING AND ENGAGING THE KEYS

The territories belong to God; therefore the keys to the territories also definitely belong to God. God Himself is the key that unlocks all things.

Keys are systems, principles, legal jurisdictions that function in the Kingdom of God. Keys make things happen. A key gives power of possession. A key gives entrance into a territory. Keys give dominion.

The First Key That Unlocks Keys-

KNOWLEDGE It is possible to be in possession of a key or keys and yet not know where or how to use them. **Knowledge** is required, so as to be able to use keys effectively and correctly. It is important to learn the keys according to the principles of God. We need to know and learn what keys are available to us, what they open and how to use them.

My people are destroyed because they have no knowledge. Hosea 4:6

It is almost impossible for a drowning man to save another drowning man while he himself is in the same drowning condition. To be able to save a drowning man successfully, one would have to be in a more advantageous position than the drowning man. **Anyone who seeks to unlock a territory would himself have to be a person unlocked.** Anyone who seeks to engage in a rescue operation must ensure that he himself is not in captivity. How can one emancipate another from a strongman while he himself is a captive of the same strongman? In unlocking any territory, one needs to ensure that one is free from chains at **all** levels.

Unlocking oneself is detangling from all that seeks to keep us shackled to darkness, ignominy, mediocrity, ineptitude, servitude, frustration and oppression. Our hearts must be positioned in the light of God. An intimate walk with Jesus is a solid place that ensures a steady flow of illumination and emancipation into one's life and destiny. We must know Jesus fully. We must know Jesus on all levels. Our relationship with God must be visible and palpable in every area of our lives, not just in some areas, every area. The knowledge of God that we have must translate into emancipation for us in every area of living.

Knowledge and understanding of your life is a key factor in unlocking yourself and unlocking your assigned territory. Do you need unlocking? Does your territory need unlocking? Which territory and why? Having a deep revelation of who you are and who God has called you to be helps you to sit down and evaluate your current situation to determine if your life is under a lock and if your assigned territory needs unlocking unto God.

There is a definite pattern of glory that God has assigned for each individual life. Aligning your life with this pattern depends on how much of God and His plans for you, you know, you understand and you embrace. God has ordained His glory for all those who are called by His name, however many children of God are living locked down and shackled lives and they have absolutely no idea, simply because it seems all their needs for sustenance are being met. Our lives are much more than food, drink, clothing and shelter. **This is a key that unlocks keys.**

The Living Word of God – The Key Owner and Holder

Jesus Christ is in full possession of the keys of all the territories. All the keys of the entire Kingdom of God, the things we see and do not see are in the hands of Jesus Christ. He is our ever present help. Jesus owns the keys, Jesus holds the keys. Jesus is the Living Key that no lock can resist.

A key is authority of access, ease of access. A key is influence, a key is control. To possess and handle keys, we must get into Jesus, we must get into the Word of God. Everything in us must conform to the word of God. You cannot hold a key upside down and expect it to work for you. We must be able to rightly divide the word of God for the word to be effective in our lives and situations.

The Second Key That Unlocks Keys-

FAITH To believe is to accept without a doubt, (especially without the occasion of proof) that something is true. The confidence that upholds a belief is rooted in respect, honour and trust for the source of that thing in which one believes. **Faith** is trust expressed in the integrity of God. We do not see, yet we believe. We do not handle physically, yet we are fully assured of its existence, its reality, its truth: this is absolute trust in the faultlessness of the word of God and in the unwavering truth that God cannot lie. Faith is trust and belief in the integrity of God. **This is a key that unlocks keys.**

so that by two unchangeable things [His promise and His oath] in which it is impossible for God to lie, we who have fled [to Him] for refuge would have strong encouragement and indwelling strength to hold tightly to the hope set before us. Hebrews 6:18

For truly, I say to you, if you have faith like a grain of mustard seed, you will say to this mountain, 'Move from here to there,' and it will move, and nothing will be impossible for you. "Matthew 17:20

For every child of God overcomes the world; and the victorious principle which has overcome the world is our faith. 1 John 5:4

Faith is beyond believing God for something in particular. Faith in God is the total surrender of one's life and destiny to the plans and purposes of God. Faith is the strong, unshakable, complete belief and trust in God, that whatever He chooses to do is right and it is perfect.

Faith is a lifestyle, a walk, a total and complete dependence on the integrity of God; that He is who He says He is and all He does is good and right and perfect; to bring you and all that concern you into His goodness. Faith in God is giving up the deep desires of your soul, your convictions, your perceptions, to embrace and live the life that Jesus has chosen for you.

The Third Key That Unlocks Keys-

Agreement. To unlock territories; there must be an ongoing relationship and conversation with God. There must be the acknowledgement that there is an assignment from God; an assignment to set into the glorious liberty of God the creation of God.

To activate an unlocking, there must be an acceptance of that assignment and an active **agreement** and engagement with the systems of emancipation that God has set into motion. **This is a powerful key that unlocks keys.**

Everyone born of God has been created for emancipation. Every child of God is a liberator, a key. As one lives and walks in agreement, in alignment and in conformity to the pattern of God, in the image and the likeness of God, it becomes clear that each individual born of God has been fashioned by God as a key to unlock lives, destinies, spheres and territories into the beauty and the glory of The Sovereign God of glory. Amen.

The word of God is the set of keys that lock and unlock territories. The power, the jurisdiction and the authority that the word of God gives to us, is the access keys that control our world. We have no power, no jurisdiction, no right of ownership, no claim to authority outside of the word of God's power. The power that speaks to creation, that upholds all things is the Word of God, His Name is Jesus. All that we are must align and agree with this truth at all times and in all things.

The Son is the radiance of God's glory and the exact expression of his nature, sustaining all things by the word of His power. Hebrews 1:3.

Exercise:

-What are the deep insights and revelations that you have received concerning your life and your assignment/s in God?

-In what specific direction do you believe that the Lord is navigating the course of your life?

-Do you believe you are ready to be used as an agent to unlock others? Would you make a success of the assignment? Why do you believe so?

-Have you learnt anything new from these articles or has your vision been honed? How?

TERRITORIAL CONSTITUTED AUTHORITY

God is Sovereign over all territories and realms; He has absolute power and authority over all. At no time at all has God been or is God inept, incapable or confused concerning anything. God is supreme in power and in authority over all. **God has chosen in Himself to delegate power and authority to regenerated man; so as to extend, expand and achieve His plans and purposes.**

God created each person for a specific purpose; He calls each saint to a specific task. God anoints each apostle for a specific territory or territories and ordains specific angels for the specific assignments.

God has ministering angels of specific purposes and territories, also anointings of specific purposes and territories that He has appointed to operate in their offices, according to His purposes and intents; to empower the saints on assignment.

So there are specific callings on specific saints, as there are specific anointings, as there are specific ministering spirits, called over persons, over assignments, over territories.

God has instituted over every territory - **territorial constituted authority** - saints empowered of God; to oversee, to occupy, to abound, to control, to manifest His plans and purposes and to rule according to His perfect will. **Territorial anointing and territorial jurisdiction** is released by God for the execution and the establishment of God's goals over the territories. Legitimate power is the basis of authority of any organisation or government. The legitimate power of God flows from God's Kingdom to bona fide citizens of the Kingdom who are in a walking and working agreement with God, who have the understanding of God's order.

As king-priests of God we are the representatives of God and also executors of justice and authoritative responsibility. However, The Holy Spirit remains the Territorial Intelligence, the Territorial Power and the Master of all spiritual transactions. He alone provides accurate territorial navigation. Viable transactions are possible only by the leading of the Spirit of the Living God. Intimate relationship in full submission to the Holy Spirit can never be over emphasised. He is the only one who sees all and knows all, His leadership and instruction is key. **This is a key.**

Your own ears will hear him. Right behind you a voice will say, "This is the way you should go," whether to the right or to the left. - Isaiah 30:21

Hearing is essential in spiritual transactions. What we hear constantly resonates in our souls and controls our lives. As we align with the plans and purposes of God in full surrender to the Holy Spirit, He takes us over and manifests in us His desires, His plans, His purposes and His power and authority over the realms of the earth. **This is a key.**

Possessing The Gates. Every territory has a gate. To enter into any territory you must first **identify and locate the gates, unlock the gates** and fully possess them. The gates are the entry points to the territory. The gates are the strength to the land. He who has authority at the gates, is in control of the territory. Gates are all about positioning. Authority is all about positioning. The Living Word of God is our position. We must discover, understand and align with our position in the word. **This is a key.**

*You should praise the LORD for his love and for the wonderful things he does for all of us. **He breaks down bronze gates and shatters iron locks.** - Psalm 107:15-16*

The first gate that must be unlocked and possessed is the gate of our understanding. (Proverbs 8; Proverbs 4:7). Understanding God's will, understanding the gates, understanding the territory, understanding the strongholds - These are all key factors in territorial conquests. **This is a key.**

By wisdom a house is built, and through understanding it is established. Proverbs 24:3

Once understanding has been possessed; the gates of the enemy do not stand a chance; for possessing the gates of the enemy is a covenant blessing from God. **This is a key.**

"... and your seed shall possess the gates of their enemies (by conquering them)." Genesis 22:17

Every one born of God is automatically positioned as a delegated authority; however, being born of God does not automatically position you as a territorial constituted authority. **Being sent** makes all the difference; this is the basic requirement for territorial anointing and authority. There is tremendous, indomitable power in **Being Sent**.

Realms Of Authority.

Authority is power to command. Authority is the right to exercise power. Authority is given to execute and to establish certain goals. Authority is power to exact obedience from others in the process of discharging the delegated responsibility. Authority is the power of rule, the power of government.

The Almighty God is the Sovereign Head of the Kingdom of God; He is God the Father, God the Son and God the Holy Spirit. All power and authority belong to Jesus. Authority flows from Jesus. He is the Author of all power, all influence and indeed all things in heaven and on earth. God is the highest authority that all in heaven and on earth must submit to. **Authority** is the governance of God.

Responsibility and Power are key to authority. Responsibility is the reason for authority. Authority is derived from responsibilities. Authority is useless outside of responsibility. Authority is given so as to carry out responsibility. Authority carries out responsibility. For everything in God, there is a purpose. Purpose defines everything created.

Purpose gives identity to everything in existence.

When there is no purpose, no responsibility; authority is unavailable. God equips with authority he whom he has given a clear cut responsibility. To be a person of authority, you must be a person of purpose – you must have a clear cut responsibility. **This is a key.**

Responsibility bestows authority. You are not entitled to authority if you do not carry a responsibility. Authority is given to those who have been given and have accepted responsibility. It is important to Identify and articulate your responsibility in the courts of God. You cannot function in any capacity of authority if you have not taken any capacity of responsibility. The level of authority you wield is tantamount to the level of responsibility that you have embraced.

God's authority is always delegated. All authority in heaven and on earth belong to God, He alone delegates authority as He pleases. No man can take responsibility or authority unto himself. You cannot exercise authority unless you have been given, nor can you embrace the

responsibility that has not been assigned to you.
This is a key.

No one elects Himself to this position of honour. He is called to it by God, as Aaron was. – Hebrew 5:4

God always releases authority that is commensurate with the responsibility given. With every God given responsibility comes the authority that has the capacity to fulfil the given responsibility in all its fullness.

Power is the force of authority. In the absence of power, authority loses its influence. Without power, authority is merely an honorary tag. Power is released for authority by the person/government that delegates the authority.

God released authority to man in the Living Word – Jesus Christ; so that man can function in the responsibility of establishing God's Kingdom on earth. Man's responsibility is to display the image of God and establish the desires of God on earth. In this general purpose, there is a variety of responsibilities, from whence each person born of God has a specific responsibility of glory. Authority is released for each task that is given.

The Authority In Purpose.

For everything under the sun, for everything in God, there is a purpose. Purpose defines everything in creation. Purpose gives identity to everything in existence. Everything in creation was created to fulfil a purpose in God. God is the author of all purpose. **God releases His authority for the manifestation of His purpose.** To engage authority, look for God's purpose. Is the unlocking of the territory in question included in the agenda of God's purpose for you? What purpose drives you in the unlocking of the territory? Divine assignment? Church assignment or personal (desire) assignment? What purpose does the territory serve in the agenda of God? Purpose is found in God, there is no purpose outside of God. God works His purpose according to His desires. Every endeavour that will succeed must follow the pattern of God's purpose, for from thence the authority and the power of God flow. **This is a key.**

*"But I have raised you up for this very purpose, that I might show you my power and that my name might be proclaimed in all the earth". –
Exodus 9:16*

Seeking For The Purpose Of God.

Seeking the Lord for His purpose and His perfect will can never be over emphasised. Many good and noble intentions have damaged and even destroyed ministries (and lives), simply because they were not of the Lord. There is a definite purpose for every life, for every entity, for every situation, for every season in creation. Everything created was created to fit a purpose in God. Every purpose has its timing and its season.

Anything that tries to manifest outside its God given purpose, or timing or season is an error. **Personal passion outside of God's purpose and God's will, will not work the authority and power of God.** We must be careful not to engage on a mission or assignment out of our own personal enthusiasm and zeal. There is always a pattern in God, seek it. Seek God for His purpose. Seek God for His timing. Seek God for His will.

For there is a time and procedure for every purpose, although the misery of man is heavy on him. Ecclesiastes 8:6

Many are the plans in a person's heart, but it is the LORD's purpose that prevails. Proverbs 19:21

No matter how good the plan looks, no matter how godly the act or the project; we must be careful to seek the Lord to be expressly led by The Holy Spirit. No matter how highly anointed we are, we must remember that we are not the Holy Spirit. Our sanctified human spirit is not the Holy Spirit. If we want to remain sons of God, then we must at every turn, in everything be (without a doubt) led by the Spirit of the Living God. Indomitable, irresistible authority and power flow from being led in purpose by the Spirit of the Living God. **This is a key.**

Authority's Power Flows From Submission.

To have a profitable understanding of authority, we must rightly understand the doctrine and discipline of submission. To function effectively in authority, you must be fully submitted to authority. To wield authority, you must yield to authority. When you yield to God's authority, God's government is imposed over you to produce His power. As you submit your soul (will, intellect, emotions) to God, to be governed by His authority, the glory of God fills you and empowers you to manifest the authority of God. **This is a key.**

We must submit to delegated or constituted authority – Leaders, employees to employers, husband & wife, to our government, and to spiritual leaders. The more we submit to God's constituted authority, the more God entrusts us with authority. Authority flows from the place of submission. Submission must be sincere, not in lip service or eye service, but in sincere heart service. When we submit sincerely to the authority that God sets up, we are submitting to God's order and God's will. **This is a key.**

For I myself am a man under authority, with soldiers under me. I tell this one, 'Go,' and he goes; and that one, 'Come,' and he comes. I say to my servant, 'Do this,' and he does it.
Matthew 8:9

Only Spirit-governed people can truly express the government of God. You cannot be self governed, sin governed or satan governed and express the government of God. When we submit our souls (will, mind, emotions,) to The Holy Spirit's authority, to be taught, guided by him and to be obedient to Him; we exercise His will, not ours. **This is a key.**

The divine order of God is expressed through us when we submit to God. The nature of Christ Jesus is the authority of God. When a believer portrays the nature of Christ, God's authority is made manifest in him. **Authority is neutralised** when one yields not to the Holy Spirit but to the flesh or the world or to satan. **This is a key.**

Exercise:

As individuals, we have spiritual, soul and bodily gateways. It is essential for us to possess our own gates and not allow them slip into the possession of the enemy.

1. What infiltrations have you noticed in your own life? Our body, for example, has five gateways: touch, taste, smell, sight and hearing. How have you been a watchman on the walls of your own gates?

   All our gateways must be subject to Jesus' authority. Defilement of any of these gateways will not only affect our lives, but also our relationship with Jesus and our assignment in Him.

2. What is your life goal? What are your short term plans? What are your long term plans?

3. What are your ears constantly tuned onto? Your dreams? Your goals? Your aspirations?

4. How has your understanding been unlocked for direction?

5. Please read the following story and <u>give your wise counsel</u> ...

"Pastor Blessing is a vibrant young man who loves the Lord. He serves the Lord diligently and passionately. He is the assistant pastor of the assembly where he serves. He is a sincere, dedicated and hardworking man of

God. The G.O of the ministry loves Pastor Blessing and his heart trusts in him.

The anointing of God on PB (as he is fondly called in the church) is very palpable, he carries the fire power of God in the word and in demonstration of power.

PB had been serving the Lord in the ministry for 17yrs and God had blessed him there with all blessings - spiritual, physical, material and human. God had even told him that he had positioned him in the ministry so as to take the vision of the work to the next level.

The ministry is a solid one. The presence and the power of God in His Spirit and His word is not only the foundation of the work, it is also the fuel that keeps the vision alive and running. The G.O. is a man of God in every true sense. There was just a slight challenge, Baba is aging. As the G.O. is getting older, his sight seems to be "dimming."

P.B. can see that the G.O.'s messages are not as sharp as before, (some pastors and elders also testified to it). The old man has started emphasising the wrong things. It is as if he does not understand that ministry work is dynamic and the times are changing rapidly. The new normal is here, and it is not church as usual. PB sees a lot of challenges ahead for the ministry, but every move he makes to effect the changes that he believes must be made now before it's too late, is being blocked or resisted by the General Overseer. Indeed, he is becoming very resistant to change and progress. It seems the elders board and the board of trustees will have to intervene at this stage."